The Human Body: Organs and Functions

PANCREAS

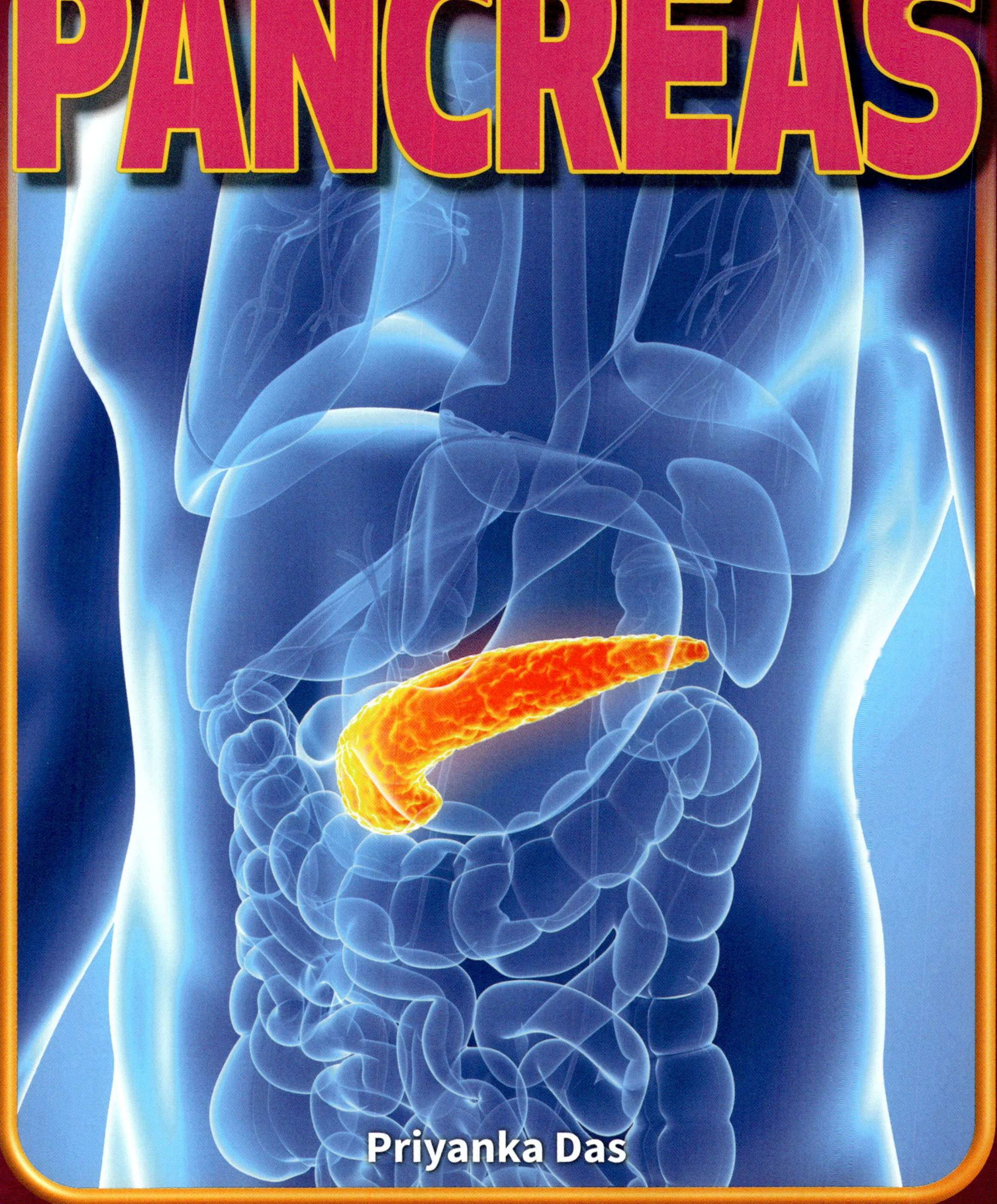

Priyanka Das

LIGHTBOX
openlightbox.com

LIGHTBOX

Go to **www.openlightbox.com** and enter this book's unique code.

ACCESS CODE

LBXK7682

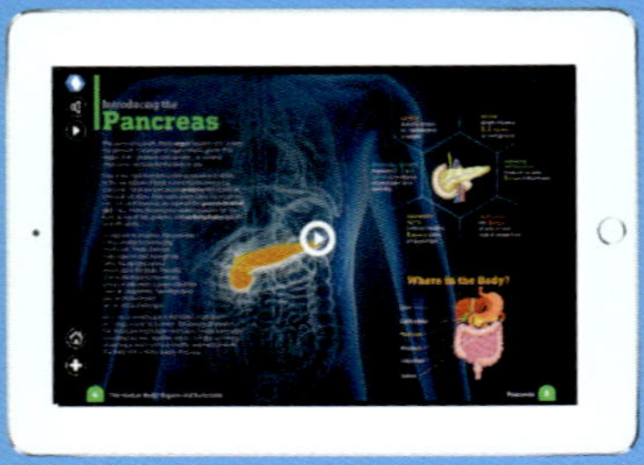

Lightbox is an all-inclusive digital solution for the teaching and learning of curriculum topics in an original, groundbreaking way. Lightbox is based on National Curriculum Standards.

LIGHTBOX SUPPLEMENTARY RESOURCES

SHARE
Share titles within your Learning Management System (LMS) or Library Circulation System

CURRICULUM
Find national and state curriculum correlations

CITATION
Create bibliographical references following APA, CMOS, and MLA styles

STANDARD FEATURES OF LIGHTBOX

AUDIO High-quality narration using text-to-speech system

ACTIVITIES Printable PDFs that can be emailed and graded

SLIDESHOWS Pictorial overviews of key concepts

VIDEOS Embedded high-definition video clips

WEBLINKS Curated links to external, child-safe resources

TRANSPARENCIES Step-by-step layering of maps, diagrams, charts, and timelines

INTERACTIVE MAPS Interactive maps and aerial satellite imagery

QUIZZES Ten multiple-choice questions that are automatically graded and emailed for teacher assessment

KEY WORDS Matching key concepts to their definitions

This title is part of our Lightbox digital subscription

Lightbox Grades 6–8 Subscription
ISBN 978-1-5105-6068-0

Access hundreds of Lightbox titles with our digital subscription. Sign up for a **FREE** subscription trial at **www.openlightbox.com/trial**

The digital components of this book are guaranteed to stay active for at least five years from the date of publication.

The Human Body: Organs and Functions

PANCREAS

CONTENTS

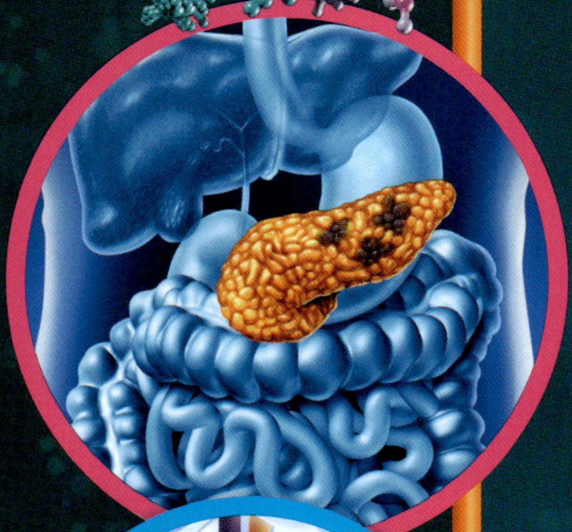

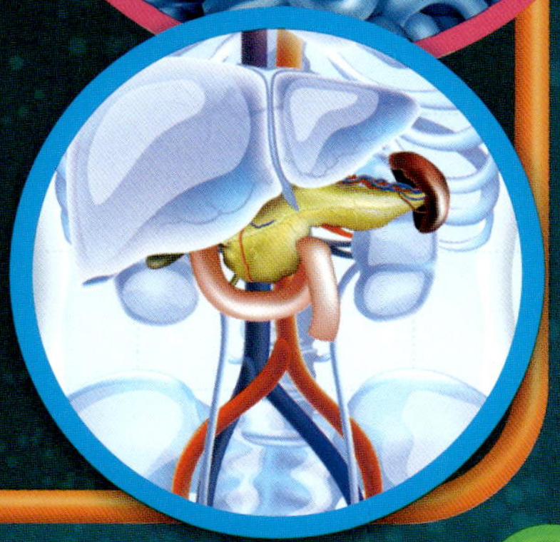

Introducing the
Pancreas

The pancreas is a soft, fleshy **organ** located behind the stomach. It is a type of organ called a gland. This means that it produces and secretes, or releases, important chemicals for the body to use.

One of the main functions of the pancreas is to assist in the breakdown of food. It does this by producing enzymes. These are specialized **proteins** that speed up chemical reactions. Pancreatic juices carry the enzymes into an organ called the small intestine. There, the enzymes make it possible for the body to **digest** fats, proteins, and **carbohydrates** quickly and efficiently.

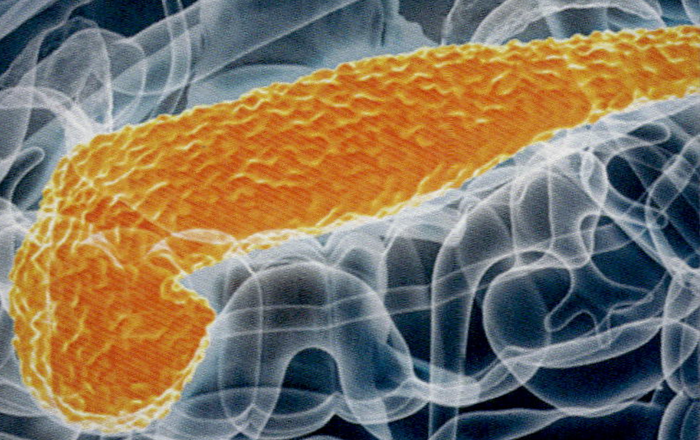

In addition to enzymes, the pancreas is responsible for producing hormones. These chemical messengers travel through the blood and regulate various processes in the body. The **cells** that make these hormones are grouped into small clusters called the islets of Langerhans.

Two of the most important hormones produced in the pancreas are insulin and glucagon. Insulin helps lower the amount of glucose in the blood, while glucagon raises glucose levels when they drop too low. Glucose, which makes up blood sugar, is the body's main source of energy. Together, insulin and glucagon keep blood sugar levels within a healthy range and provide the body with a stable supply of energy.

LENGTH
About **6** inches
(15 centimeters)

WEIGHT
Roughly **0.2** pounds
(0.1 kilograms)

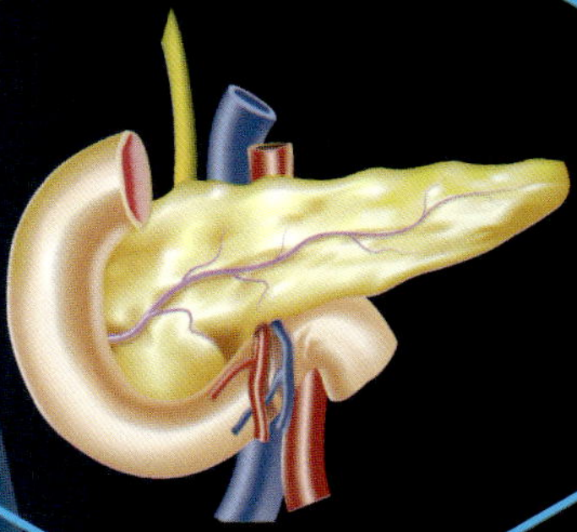

RELEASING ENZYMES
Makes **0.3** to **1** gallons (1 to 4 liters) of pancreatic juice each day

HORMONE PRODUCTION
Produces at least **5** types of hormones

PANCREATIC ISLETS
Roughly **1** million islets of Langerhans

ISLET CELLS
6 types of cells in each islet of Langerhans

Where in the Body?

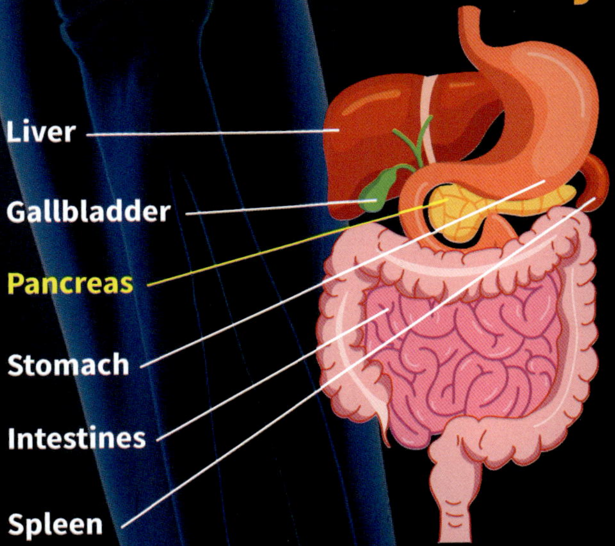

The Body's Organ Systems

The human body's 78 organs work together in organ systems. There are 11 major organ systems that control everything from movement and digestion to breathing, circulation, and internal communication. Most organs belong to a single organ system. The pancreas, however, has a dual role. It is part of both the digestive and endocrine systems.

In the digestive system, the pancreas functions as an accessory organ. This means it is not part of the the **gastrointestinal (GI) tract** and does not directly touch food. Instead, the pancreatic juices it produces travel through a tube called the pancreatic duct to reach the small intestine.

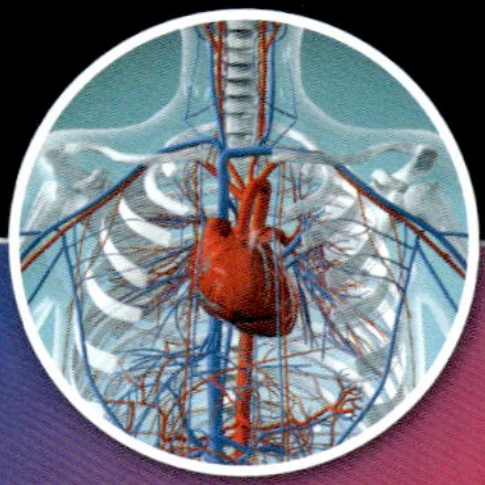

Circulatory System
Transports blood, moving substances to and from the body's cells

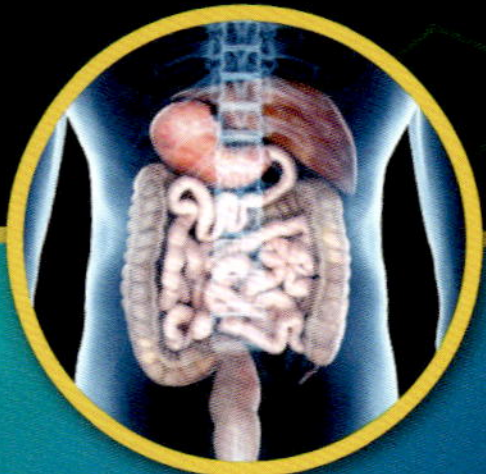

Digestive System
Extracts energy and **nutrients** from food

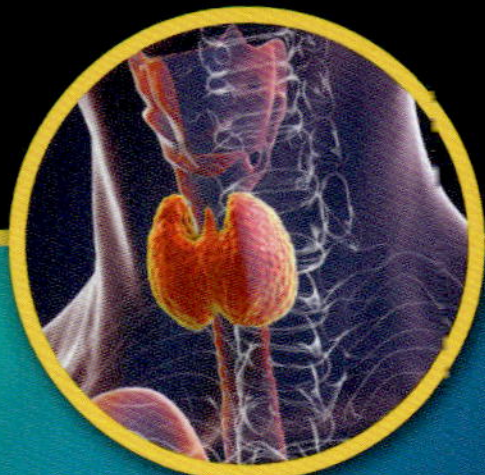

Endocrine System
Controls the release of hormones and maintains **homeostasis**

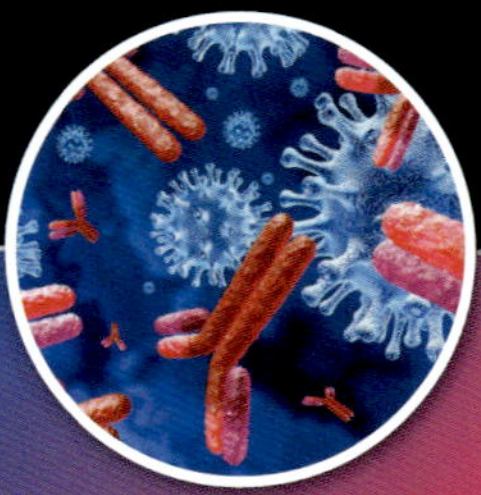

Immune System
Protects the body from attack by **pathogens**

Integumentary System
Protects the internal organs and is primarily made up of skin

Muscular System
Works together with the skeletal system to allow the body to move

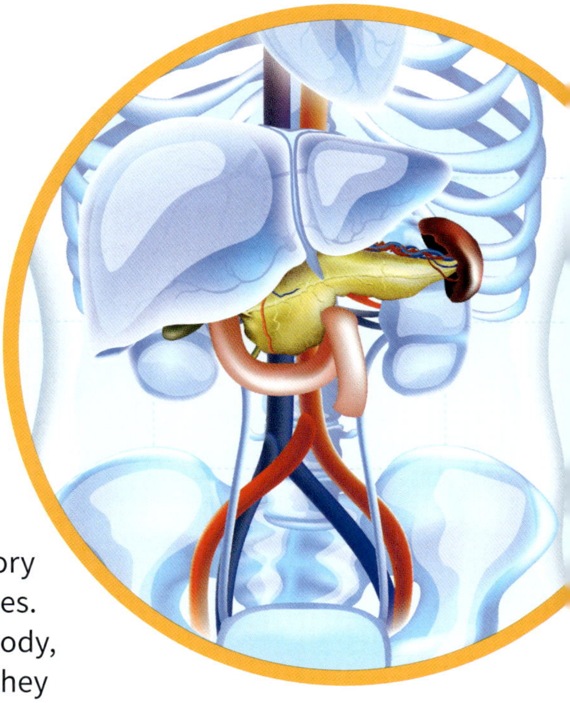

As part of the endocrine system, the pancreas helps maintain homeostasis inside the body. It monitors blood conditions and adjusts hormone levels to match the body's needs. The pancreas responds quickly to changes in blood sugar to help the body stay balanced during meals, sleep, physical activity, and periods of stress.

When the pancreas produces insulin or glucagon, it releases them directly into the blood. The circulatory system acts as the delivery system for these hormones. **Blood vessels** carry the hormones throughout the body, where they signal organs and tissues to adjust how they use or store energy.

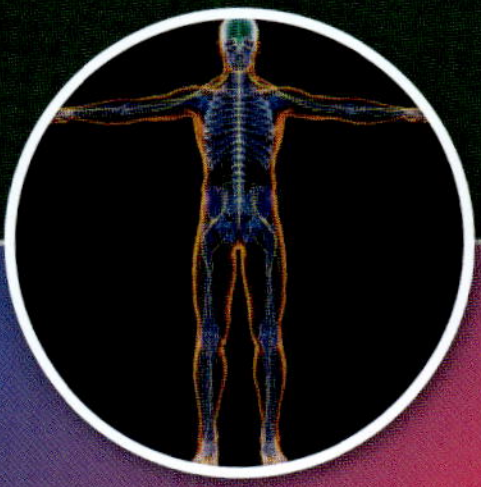

Nervous System
Carries signals between the brain and the rest of the body

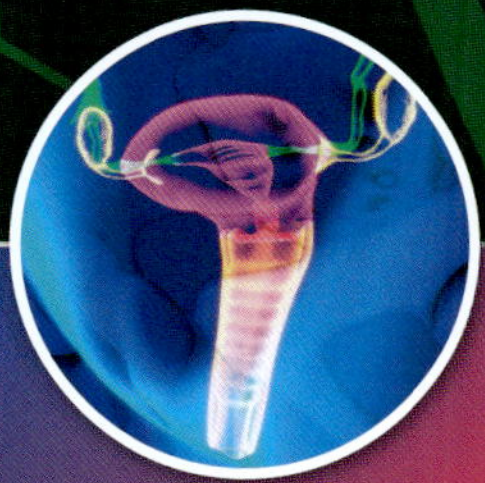

Reproductive System
Enables people to have children

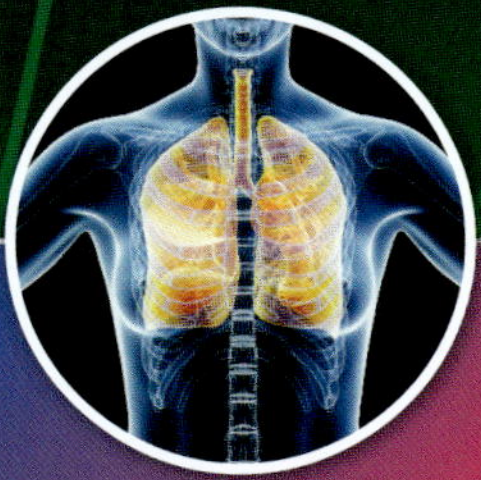

Respiratory System
Removes carbon dioxide from the body and takes in oxygen

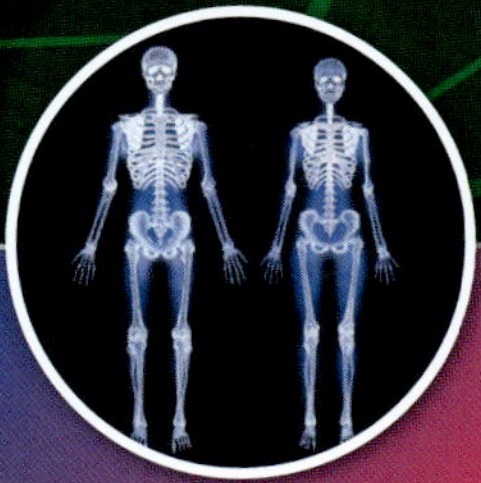

Skeletal System
Supports the body and protects the internal organs

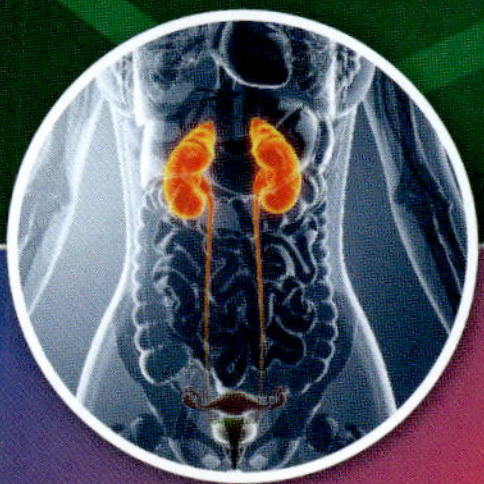

Urinary System
Filters blood, removing excess water and some waste products

Structure of the Pancreas

The pancreas has a long, flat shape. Its four main parts are its wide head, short neck, tapering body, and narrow tail. The head is nestled in the curve of the duodenum, the first part of the small intestine. Next to the head is the neck. The body, the largest part, extends horizontally between the neck and the tail, which stretches toward an organ called the spleen.

The pancreas contains many small ducts that join together to form the pancreatic duct. This duct then merges with the **common bile duct** near the duodenum. Together, these two ducts release bile and pancreatic juices into the small intestine.

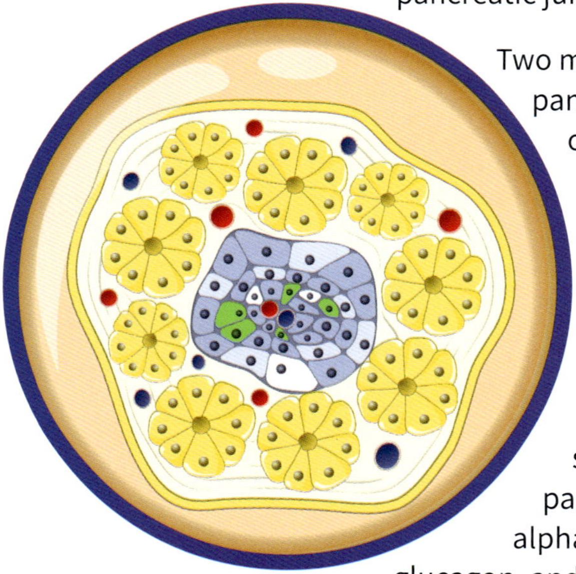

Two main types of tissue make up the pancreas. About 95 percent of the organ is **exocrine** tissue arranged in clusters called acini. These contain acinar cells that make and store digestive enzymes. The rest of the pancreas is endocrine tissue, which is what contains the islets of Langerhans. The islets are scattered throughout the pancreas. Each islet contains alpha cells, which make glucagon, and beta cells, which produce insulin. Other types of cells in the islets produce additional hormones that help regulate digestion and energy use.

One of the main organs that insulin and glucagon send signals to is the liver, which stores much of the body's glucose in a form called glycogen. If the liver detects insulin, it begins converting extra glucose from the blood into glycogen to lower blood sugar levels. When the pancreas releases glucagon, the liver breaks down its glycogen stores and releases glucose back into the blood to raise blood sugar levels.

Pancreas Anatomy

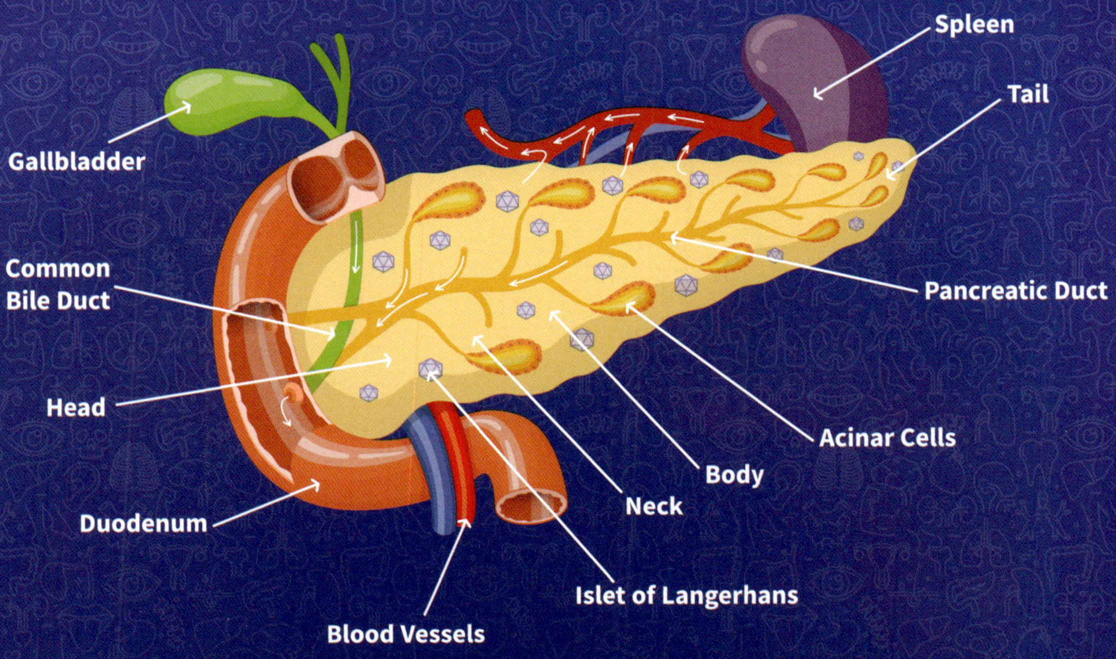

Blood Sugar Levels

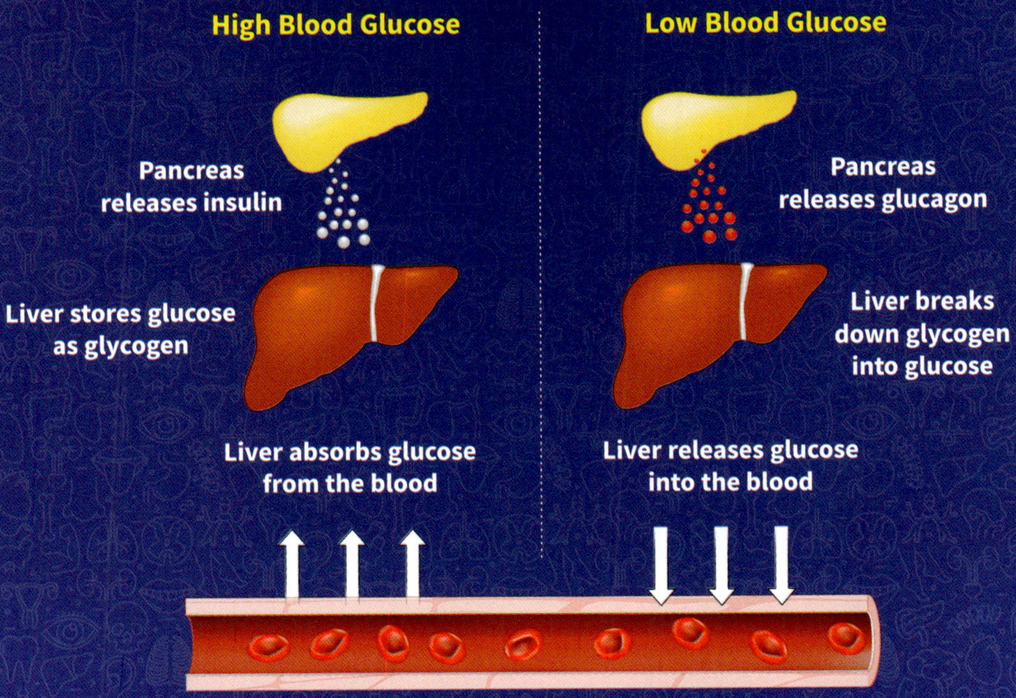

Role in the Body

With both exocrine and endocrine functions, the pancreas is a unique organ. In its endocrine role, it regulates the glucose that the body's cells need in order to function. Its exocrine function is to help the digestive system break down food into nutrients that the body can absorb.

Reducing Blood Sugar Levels

After a meal, the amount of glucose in the blood rises. This is because the body is digesting and absorbing carbohydrates, which break down into glucose. The pancreas releases insulin in response. Insulin signals cells throughout the body, especially in the **skeletal muscles** and liver, to take in glucose from the blood and either use it for energy or store it as glycogen. As glucose is absorbed, blood sugar levels return to normal.

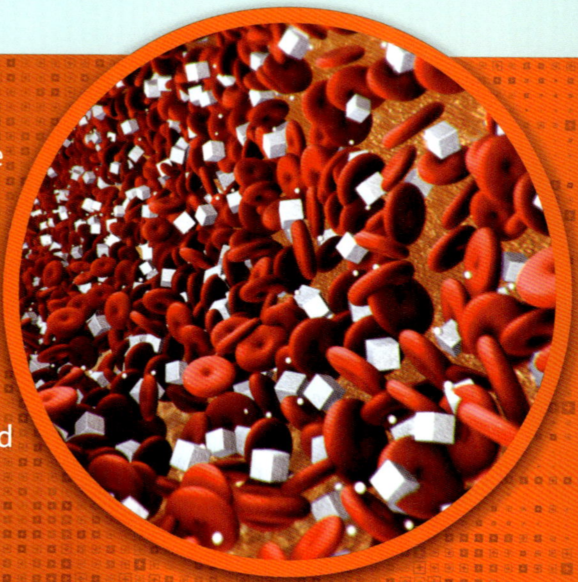

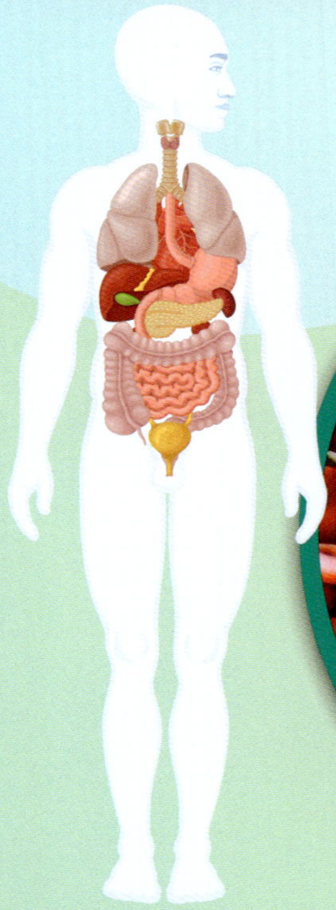

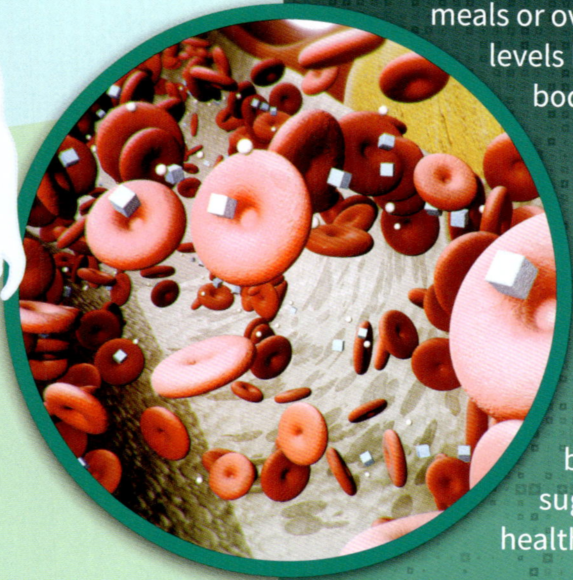

Increasing Blood Sugar Levels

During periods of fasting, such as between meals or overnight, blood sugar levels begin to fall. To keep the body supplied with energy in this fasting state, the pancreas releases glucagon. This signals the liver to break down stored glycogen into glucose. The newly released glucose enters the blood, raising blood sugar levels back to a healthy range.

Storing and Releasing Digestive Enzymes

Pancreatic cells make enzymes in an inactive form. Known as zymogens, they are only activated once they reach the small intestine. This prevents the pancreas from digesting itself and enzymes from being used up. Pancreatic enzymes include amylases, lipases, and proteases, which break down different types of food.

Neutralizing Stomach Acid

The stomach contains a strong chemical called hydrochloric acid. It makes the food that leaves the stomach very acidic. To allow the enzymes it releases to work properly and to protect the small intestine from stomach acid, the pancreas releases a substance called bicarbonate. This neutralizes stomach acid, creating the right conditions for digestion to continue.

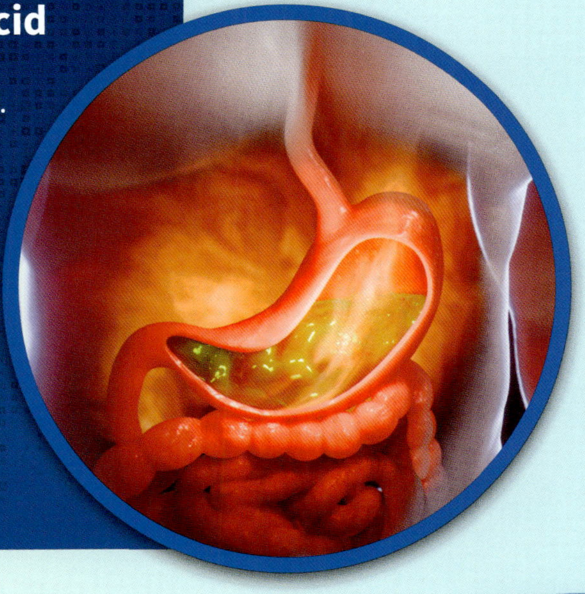

Can You Live Without It? YES!

The pancreas is not one of the body's five vital organs. This means it is possible to live without it. However, the functions it performs are essential for long-term health. A pancreatectomy, or the surgical removal of all or part of the pancreas, is only performed as a last resort. The most common reason for a pancreatectomy is pancreatic cancer. After surgery, careful medical support and lifestyle changes are needed. A person must take enzyme pills to help digest food and insulin to control blood sugar.

A Medical Timeline

Scientific knowledge about the pancreas has developed over thousands of years. Early observations focused on its structure, while later discoveries have been related to its functions. Today, two branches of medicine that study the pancreas are **gastroenterology** and **endocrinology**.

circa 300 BC

Herophilus, an ancient Greek surgeon, becomes the first person to describe the pancreas.

circa 100 AD

The Greek physician **Rufus of Ephesus** names the pancreas. He calls it *pánkreas*, which means "all flesh."

circa 200

In Rome, the physician **Galen** includes the pancreas in his anatomical writings. He believes the organ provides structural support to nearby blood vessels.

1642

Johann Georg Wirsung, a German **anatomist**, discovers the pancreatic duct while dissecting a human body. Today, the pancreatic duct is also known as the "**duct of Wirsung**" in his honor.

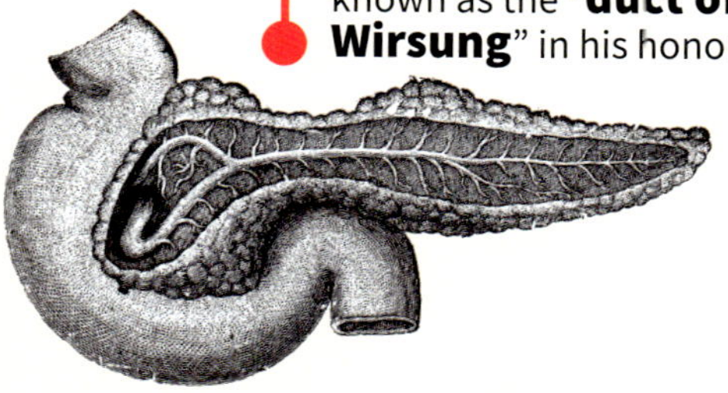

1869

German medical student **Paul Langerhans** discovers the islets of Langerhans.

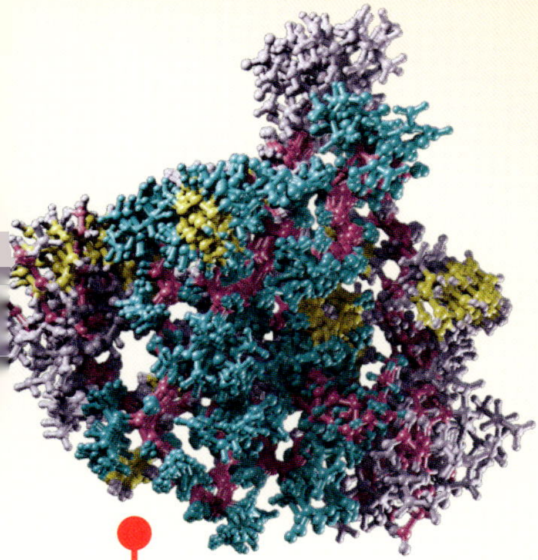

1921

At the University of Toronto, in Canada, Frederick Banting and his student, Charles Best, **discover insulin**.

1958

British biochemist **Frederick Sanger** is awarded the **Nobel Prize** in Chemistry for his work determining the structure of insulin.

2009

The U.S. Food and Drug Administration (FDA) approves the use of Pancreatic Enzyme Replacement Therapy (PERT), or **enzyme pills**.

2023

Artificial intelligence (AI) is used to successfully identify people who are at high risk of developing pancreatic cancer.

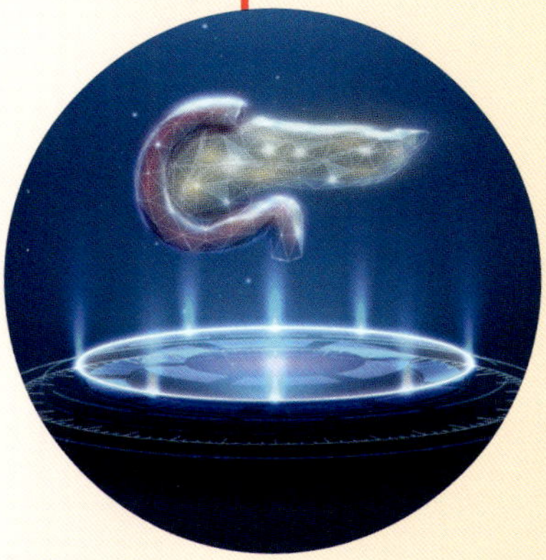

2025

Scientists research ways to restore proper function in damaged **pancreatic cells**, especially the beta cells that produce insulin.

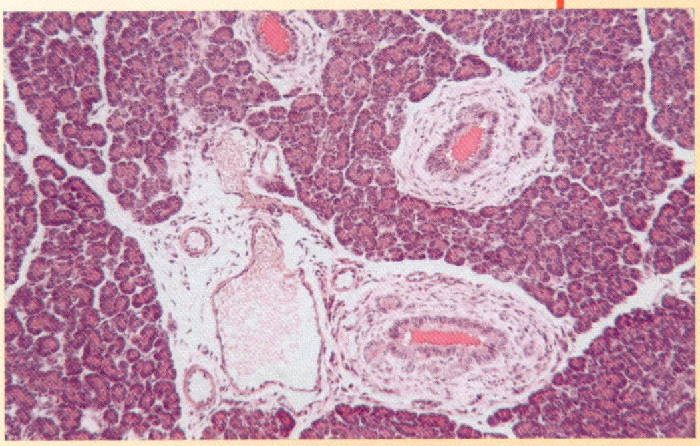

Organs Working Together

In its role helping the digestive and endocrine systems, the pancreas works closely with other key organs. The brain, liver, and skeletal muscles help the pancreas regulate glucose levels. The small intestine receives the pancreatic enzymes, while the gallbladder secretes bile to help the lipases.

The Pancreas works with the...

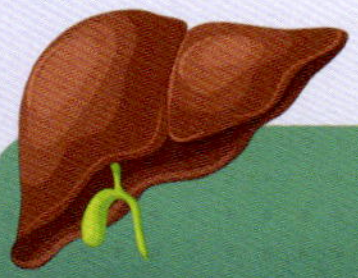

Liver to Control Blood Sugar

- Blood sugar rises after eating
- Pancreas releases insulin
- Insulin signals liver to store glucose as glycogen
- Blood sugar levels fall

- Blood sugar drops between meals
- Pancreas releases glucagon
- Glucagon signals liver to release glucose into blood
- Blood sugar levels rise

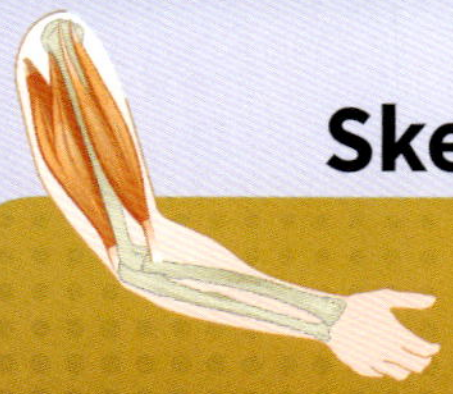

Skeletal Muscles to Control Blood Sugar

- Blood sugar rises after eating
- Pancreas releases insulin
- Insulin signals muscle cells to absorb glucose from blood
- Muscles use glucose for energy or store it as glycogen

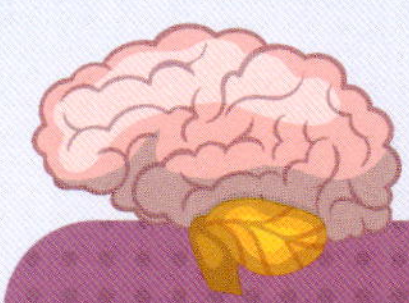

Brain to Regulate Hormones

Brain monitors blood sugar levels → Brain sends signals to pancreas if blood sugar levels need to change → Pancreas adjusts hormone levels in response → Blood sugar stabilizes to meet the body's needs

Small Intestine to Digest Food

Food enters small intestine → Small intestine releases a hormone called cholecystokinin (CCK) → CCK signals pancreas to release digestive enzymes → Lipases, amylases, and proteases travel through pancreatic duct to small intestine

Lipase breaks down…

Fats → Fatty acids and glycerol

Amylase breaks down…

Carbohydrates → Glucose

Protease breaks down…

Proteins → Amino acids

Gallbladder to Digest Fats

Food enters small intestine, causing it to release CCK → CCK signals pancreas to release enzymes and gallbladder to release bile → Ducts transport pancreatic enzymes and bile into small intestine → Bile increases surface area of fats so lipase is able to break them down faster

Diseases of the Pancreas

When the pancreas is not functioning properly, it can lead to serious health problems. Pancreatic diseases may affect the production of digestive enzymes or the release of hormones that control blood sugar. These conditions can interfere with digestion, cause pain, and lead to long-term complications if not treated early.

Type 1 Diabetes

Type 1 diabetes is an autoimmune condition, which means that the body's immune system attacks itself. In type 1 diabetes, the immune system destroys the insulin-producing beta cells in the pancreas. Without insulin, blood sugar levels become dangerously high. Over time, high blood sugar damages blood vessels and **nerves**. Type 1 diabetes usually develops in children or teenagers and requires daily insulin treatment.

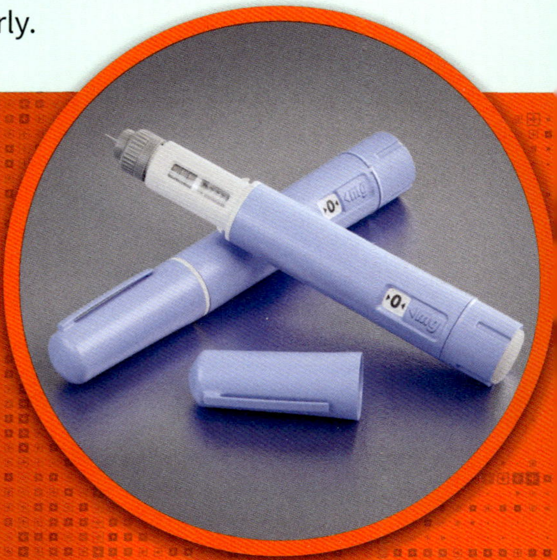

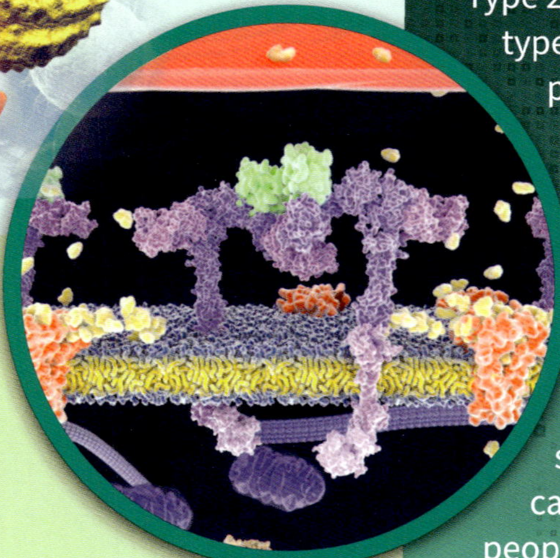

Type 2 Diabetes

Type 2 diabetes is more common than type 1 diabetes. It occurs when the pancreas does not produce enough insulin or when the body stops responding properly to insulin. Type 2 diabetes is found more often in adults than in children. It is often linked to poor diet, being overweight, and lack of physical activity. Healthy habits, such as lifestyle and diet changes, can help manage the disease. Many people with type 2 diabetes need to take insulin treatments.

Pancreatitis

Pancreatitis is **inflammation** of the pancreas. This condition occurs when digestive enzymes become active while still inside the pancreas, causing the organ to begin digesting itself. Pancreatitis can be acute or chronic. Acute pancreatitis is sudden and temporary, while chronic pancreatitis is a long-term disease. Symptoms of pancreatitis include severe abdominal pain, nausea, vomiting, and fever.

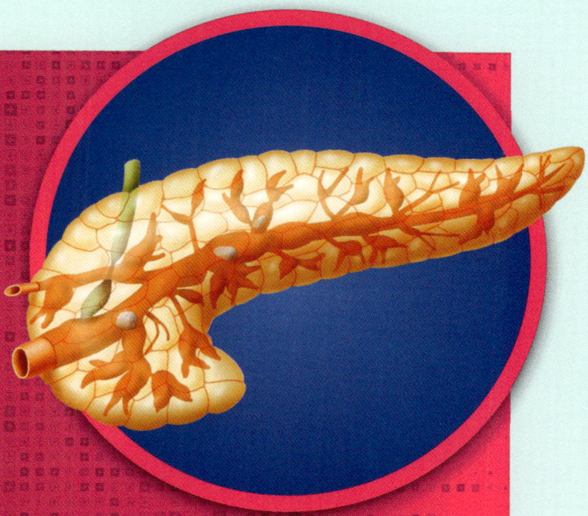

Pancreatic Cancer

Pancreatic cancer occurs when abnormal cells form a mass called a tumor in the pancreas. This disease is often difficult to detect in its early stages and may not cause symptoms until it has spread. Stomach or back pain, weight loss, **jaundice**, and a lack of appetite are some symptoms of pancreatic cancer.

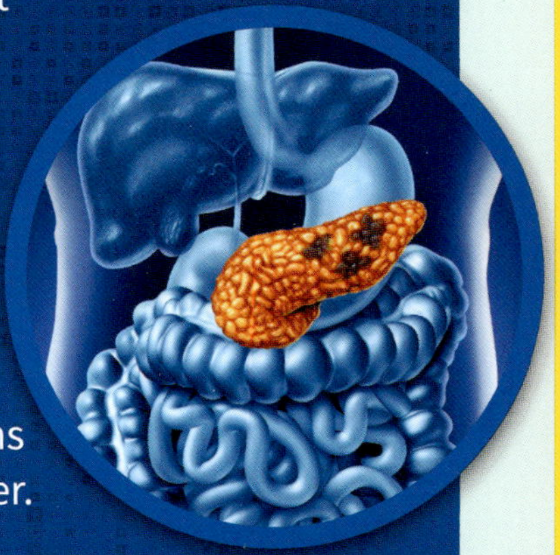

Warning Signs!

Certain symptoms may point to problems with the pancreas. If these signs appear, it is important to go to a doctor right away.

- Abdominal pain
- Back pain
- Unexplained weight loss
- Nausea or vomiting
- Jaundice
- Loss of appetite
- Fatigue, or feeling tired and unwell
- Increased thirst
- Frequent urination
- Dark urine
- Pale or greasy stool

Low and High Blood Sugar

When the amount of glucose in the blood drops too low, it is called hypoglycemia. If the levels of blood glucose rise too high, it is known as hyperglycemia. Both conditions are more common in people with diabetes.

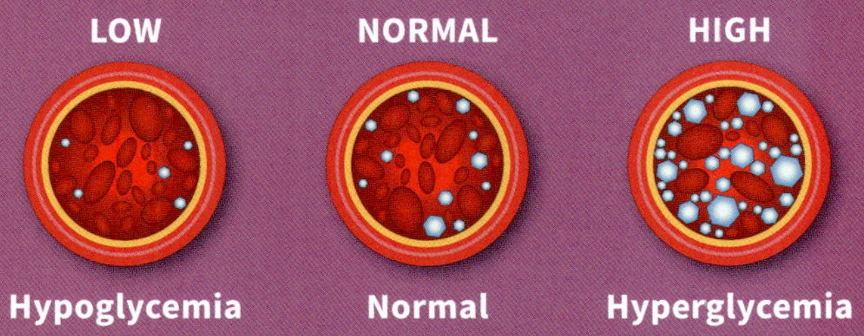

Medicine around the World

Across the globe, scientists and doctors are studying the pancreas and the hormones and enzymes it produces. Hospitals, universities, and research centers play major roles in finding new ways to treat pancreatic disorders. While gastroenterology departments usually treat diseases such as pancreatitis, diabetes falls under the field of endocrinology.

Joslin Diabetes Center, United States

1

The Joslin Diabetes Center, in Boston, is the largest diabetes research center in the world. Its researchers focus entirely on diabetes treatment and research. The center studies how insulin is produced and how pancreatic beta cells function. It is also developing new drugs to protect these cells from damage.

University of Toronto, Canada

2

When Frederick Banting and Charles Best discovered insulin in 1921, they did it by extracting the hormone from a dog's pancreas. Their work led to the development of life-saving treatments for diabetes. They also earned international recognition, and Banting was awarded the Nobel Prize in Physiology or Medicine in 1923. Today, the Banting & Best Diabetes Centre at the University of Toronto is a leader in diabetes research and education.

Christian Medical College, India

3

Christian Medical College, in Vellore, treats thousands of patients with diabetes and pancreatitis each year. Its hospital combines modern **diagnostics** with low-cost treatment options. It also trains doctors to provide pancreas-related care in underserved regions.

Kyoto University, Japan

4

Kyoto University is working on new methods to **screen** for pancreatic cancer, which is often treatable when detected early. However, since the disease often does not have any symptoms in its early stages, it is usually not discovered until the cancer has progressed to an advanced state. Using AI to examine data, researchers at Kyoto University are exploring ways to improve early detection of pancreatic cancer.

What is an Endocrinologist?

Doctors who specialize in hormones and the glands that produce them are called endocrinologists. They diagnose and treat conditions such as type 1 and type 2 diabetes. Endocrinologists may order blood tests and use tools to check how well the pancreas and other glands are working. These doctors often work with patients over a long period of time to monitor blood sugar, adjust medications, and give advice on healthy habits.

Keeping the Pancreas Healthy

More than 30 million people in the United States have type 2 diabetes. Practicing healthy habits from a young age can help prevent this and other pancreas-related diseases. Good nutrition, **hydration**, and exercise protect the pancreas and help it work properly.

TIP 1

Eat Fruits, Vegetables, and Whole Grains

Fruits and vegetables are rich in **micronutrients**, water, and fiber. These help the pancreas and the rest of the body stay strong. Foods such as brown rice, oats, and whole wheat bread also contain fiber and improve digestion.

TIP 2

Limit Sugary Foods and Refined Carbohydrates

Too much sugar makes the pancreas work harder and can damage it over time. Avoiding sugary drinks and eating less white bread, white rice, sweets, and desserts helps prevent problems later on.

TIP 3

Stay Active

Exercise helps the body use glucose for energy. Walking, running, dancing, and playing sports are all good ways to keep active.

TIP 4

Stay Hydrated

Water keeps the body hydrated and supports the pancreas as it makes digestive juices. Aim to drink water instead of sugary drinks.

TIP 5

Eat Regular Meals

Skipping meals or eating too much at once can affect how the pancreas releases enzymes and insulin. Eating regular, balanced meals is better for the body.

Activity: Enzymes at Work

The pancreas is not the only organ that makes enzymes. Cells throughout the body use enzymes to speed up reactions. Digestive enzymes are also found in plants and animals. For example, fresh pineapples contain an enzyme called bromelain. Try the activity below to see what this enzyme does.

Materials

- Fresh pineapple cut into chunks
- Gelatin powder
- Water
- Measuring cup
- Large bowl
- Two cups that are the same size
- Spoon

Steps

1. Prepare the Gelatin: Mix the gelatin powder and water in the bowl according to the instructions on the package. Since gelatin is made out of an animal protein called collagen, it represents the proteins in food.

2. Let it Cool: If the instructions on the gelatin package tell you to use warm or hot water, wait a few minutes for the mixture to cool slightly. High temperatures denature, or destroy, most enzymes.

3. Pour the Gelatin: Use the measuring cup to help you pour equal amounts of gelatin into each of the two cups.

4. Add Pineapple Chunks: Add a few chunks of pineapple to one of the cups. This step must be done with a fresh pineapple, since the bromelain in canned pineapple is denatured.

5. Refrigerate the Cups: Place both the cups into a refrigerator. Write down your hypothesis, or educated guess, about what will happen to the gelatin in each cup. Wait for about four hours to give the gelatin time to set.

6. Observe the Gelatin: After four hours, remove the cups from the refrigerator. Do their contents look different? Write down what you notice about the **texture** of the gelatin in each cup. The mixture in the bowl with only gelatin should be solid, while the mixture that includes the pineapple chunks should be more watery.

7. Analyze and Discuss: Gelatin sets because its collagen proteins stick together. The bromelain in pineapple is a type of protease. It breaks the collagen in gelatin apart, causing the gelatin to lose its shape. Discuss what this helps you understand about the role of proteases and other enzymes in digestion.

Quiz

1
What are enzymes in their inactive form called?

2
How does the pancreas neutralize stomach acid?

3
Which two branches of medicine study the pancreas?

4
What are enzymes?

5
Who discovered insulin?

6
Which pancreatic hormone raises blood glucose?

7
What is the more common type of diabetes?

8
Which enzymes break up carbohydrates?

9
Which pancreatic hormone lowers blood glucose?

10
What does the word *pánkreas* mean?

ANSWERS

1. Zymogens **2.** By releasing bicarbonate **3.** Gastroenterology and endocrinology **4.** Specialized proteins that speed up chemical reactions **5.** Frederick Banting and Charles Best **6.** Glucagon **7.** Type 2 diabetes **8.** Amylases **9.** Insulin **10.** "All flesh"

Key Words

anatomist: a scientist who studies the structure of the human body

blood vessels: tubes that carry blood throughout the body

carbohydrates: nutrients found in foods such as bread, pasta, and rice

cells: the smallest structural and functional units of living organisms

common bile duct: a tube that carries bile, a greenish-yellow digestive fluid that helps break down fats, from the liver and gallbladder to the small intestine

diagnostics: tools or tests used to identify a disease or condition

digest: to break down food into a form that the body is able to absorb

endocrinology: the branch of medicine that studies hormones and glands

exocrine: relating to glands that release substances through ducts instead of blood vessels

gastroenterology: the branch of medicine focused on the digestive system

gastrointestinal (GI) tract: a long, continuous tube that runs from the mouth to anus and contains hollow digestive organs

homeostasis: the body's ability to maintain a stable internal environment despite external changes

hydration: drinking enough water to keep the body healthy and functioning well

inflammation: the body's response to injury or infection, often resulting in redness, swelling, heat, or pain

jaundice: a condition that causes yellowing of the skin and eyes

micronutrients: substances that the body needs in very small amounts, such as vitamins and minerals

nerves: bundles of fibers that carry signals between the brain and the rest of the body

Nobel Prize: a prestigious international award given for outstanding achievements in science, literature, or peace

nutrients: substances found in food that provide energy for the body to use

organ: a distinct structure in the body that is made up of tissues and performs one or more specific functions

pathogens: microorganisms, such as bacteria or viruses, that cause diseases

proteins: nutrients found in foods such as meat, fish, and eggs

screen: a medical test used to check for a disease before symptoms appear

skeletal muscles: muscles attached to bones that help the body move

texture: the way something feels or looks

Index

LIGHTBOX

SUPPLEMENTARY RESOURCES

Click on the plus icon found in the bottom left corner of each spread to open additional teacher resources.

- Download and print the book's quizzes and activities
- Access curriculum correlations
- Explore additional web applications that enhance the Lightbox experience

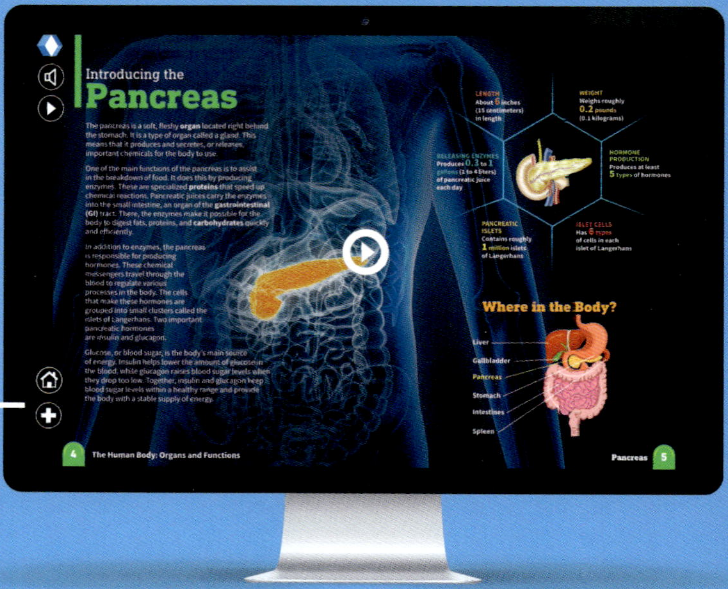

LIGHTBOX DIGITAL TITLES

Packed full of integrated media

VIDEOS

INTERACTIVE MAPS

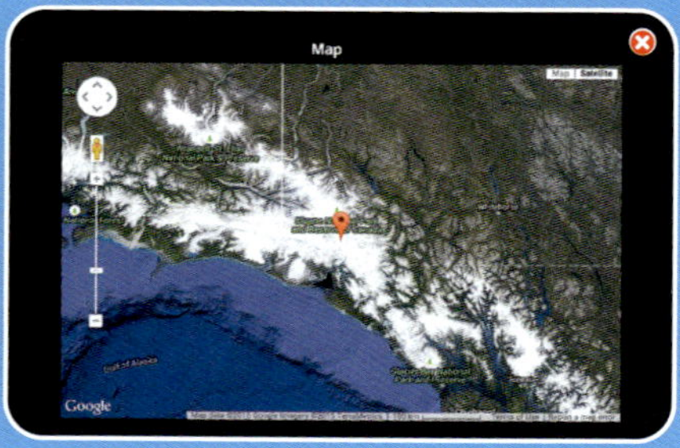

WEBLINKS

SLIDESHOWS

QUIZZES

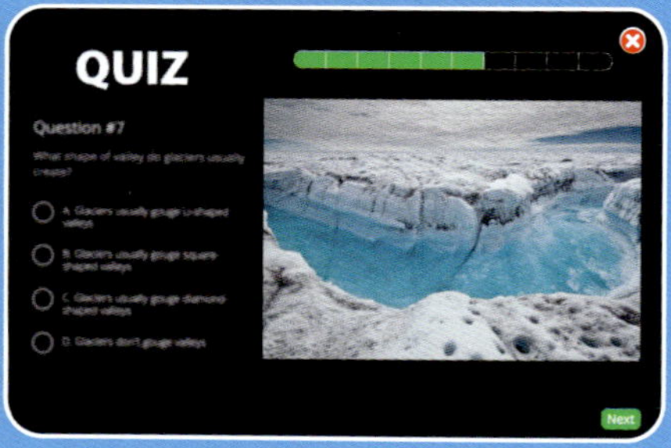

OPTIMIZED FOR

- ✓ TABLETS
- ✓ SMART BOARDS
- ✓ COMPUTERS
- ✓ AND MUCH MORE!

Published by Lightbox Learning Inc.
276 5th Avenue, Suite 704 #917
New York, NY 10001
Website: www.openlightbox.com

Library of Congress Control Number: 2025932680

ISBN 978-1-5105-8685-7 (hardcover)
ISBN 978-1-5105-8686-4 (static multi-user eBook)
ISBN 978-1-5105-8688-8 (interactive multi-user eBook)

Printed in Fargo, North Dakota, in the United States of America
1 2 3 4 5 6 7 8 9 0 29 28 27 26 25

082025
111024

Project Coordinator: Priyanka Das
Design: Jean Faye Rodriguez